Key Truths
FOR WOMEN
Essentials for Spiritual Growth

Key Truths
FOR WOMEN
Essentials for Spiritual Growth

MARTHA TYLER

REGULAR BAPTIST PRESS
1300 North Meacham Road
Schaumburg, Illinois 60173-4806

KEY TRUTHS FOR WOMEN:
ESSENTIALS FOR SPIRITUAL GROWTH
© 2005
Regular Baptist Press • Schaumburg, Illinois
www.RegularBaptistPress.org • 1-800-727-4440
Printed in U.S.A.
RBP5323 • ISBN: 978-1-59402-226-5
Second printing—2008

Contents

Dedication

To my grandchildren,
whom I love dearly:
David, Jacquelyn,
Leah, Barbara,
and Sarah.
I hope and pray they
make their lives count
for God.

Preface

ON MAY 8, 2002, my life came to a screeching halt. My husband went Home to be with the Lord, and my marriage of almost forty-five years ended forever. I was devastated! After a few weeks of feeling stunned, I began to ask myself some questions: What is God teaching me through this experience? What do I need to learn? What does God have for me in the future? Little by little my Lord began to help me. I began to feel like joining the human race again; I began to feel as if I could live again and not merely exist.

God helped me change my whole perspective on life; He helped me want to be used by Him in the future. I realized how short life actually is and how only the things done for God really count (even though I'd known this fact most of my life). In the past I had my whole life planned; now I could only trust God to lead me day-by-day and step-by-step.

Although I had started this study before my husband died, I finished it afterwards, writing out of the depths of my heart as a means to encourage myself. I hope it will encourage you as well and will help you develop your spiritual maturity and meet whatever needs you face.

Most of the topics came from my husband's sermons. I took these topics and put them into key words, words that will help you unlock your potential for spiritual growth.

My prayer is that these lessons will instruct you concerning the true meaning of these important words, will move you to respond to their claims, and will propel you to apply them to your life. As a result, you will, I trust, be motivated to make your life count for Christ!

How to Lower Your Temper[ature]

Key Word: Anger

"He that is slow to anger is better than the mighty; and he that ruleth his spirit than he that taketh a city" *(Proverbs 16:32).*

AN ANGRY WIFE placed an ad in a newspaper that read, "Used wedding dress for sale—will trade for a .38 caliber pistol." We, like that woman, find anger sneaking its way into our lives. Everyone has experienced it and been affected by it.

One person defined anger as a towering giant we never conquer. But anger can be an appropriate response to injustice or sin. However, when it is unchecked or misdirected, it can cause great destruction. Even if we justify our anger, our rationalization does not make it right.

Although anger is ages old, it has become a major problem. The Bible teaches that unresolved anger and resentment are as serious as murder. Anger is the root of many crimes, as well as the cause of family problems and much of the stress we face today.

Anger takes many forms and may unconsciously be hidden as smoldering resentment or covered hurt. Inward anger seems to be the most destructive. Anger takes our focus off God and sets us on a course toward evil.

Anger comes with high costs. It can do more harm to the vessel in which it is *stored* than to the vessel on which it is *poured.* We are never more vulnerable than when we are angry. Anger lowers our self-control and decreases our power of reason, thus causing our common sense to forsake us. As a result, many hurtful words come out of our mouths—words that can damage our mates, our children, and the people we love and respect the most. Whether we vent our anger by silence, rage, or temper tantrums, we use our energy in unproductive, ungodly ways.

I trust that this lesson will first help us perceive anger from God's viewpoint and second help us, by God's grace, to start controlling our anger. May God help us start anew today!

Unlocking the Truths about Anger

What is anger? It is a hostile emotion that brings displeasure either to us or to someone else. People who study anger tell us there are at least five different levels of anger, with each one more intense than the previous one.

⇨ The mildest form of anger is irritation. It is a mild, provoking annoyance.

⇨ The next level is a little more emotional. The cause of our anger at this level hurts our pride and dignity. It makes us want to express anger in some small way. This level is associated with righteous anger.

⇨ The next level of anger is more intense and not only makes us feel that we must express our anger but also that we must avenge our anger.

⇨ As anger intensifies, it becomes furious, uncontrolled, and more violent. It becomes wild rage.

⇨ The last level, in which anger goes unchecked, is the most dangerous. At this level the angry person temporarily loses self-control, possibly even before he or she realizes it.

Now that we have looked at the various levels of anger, let's look at what God says about anger.

The Bible mentions God's anger (for example, Psalm 103:9). But there is a difference between God's anger and the temper tantrums we throw. In the Bible God's anger was not about things relating only to Him. Even when God became angry with Israel and others who opposed Him, it was because He loved them and wanted the best—holiness and obedience—for them. So God directed His anger toward sin, abuse, and un-godliness. God's anger is unselfish; it reflects His commitment to righteousness. We hardly ever become angry about these things; we tend to tolerate them.

Is it possible to have sinless anger? Yes. Most people are surprised to learn that anger can have a righteous effect. When is it okay to be angry? It is okay to be angry when anger is motivated by love; for example, when a sister in Christ is openly and knowingly disobeying the Word of God. This anger is constructive. However, we are not dealing with constructive, righteously motivated anger in this lesson but with anger that results from self-centeredness.

God has set up some clear instructions to help us handle anger.

1. Read Ephesians 4:26. How are we to deal with anger?

One comedian jokingly interpreted this principle as, "Don't go to bed angry; stay up and fight!" However, we must not allow ourselves the luxury of nursing our anger. When we postpone dealing with it, we lick our wounds and, usually, hurt *only* ourselves. Our anger becomes a grudge that in the end turns into poison and bitterness. It eats away at our emotional well-being. God says that we should not let the problem linger but should solve it by the end of the day. Anger never gets better. The longer we nurse it, the worse it becomes.

Ephesians 4:27 continues the thought of verse 26. The words "give place to the devil" mean to give the Devil an opportunity in our lives.

2. Read Ephesians 4:27. What happens when we hold on to our anger?

When we open our hearts to anger and wrath, we open the door for Satan to move into our lives with things even worse than anger. We can compare anger to wet cement: it's easy to get into, but you must get out of it before it hardens. When anger hardens, it turns into bitterness. So we need to deal with anger immediately.

In addition to not nursing our anger, we must not rehearse it. Have you ever been around someone who loves to tell you why she is angry? Each time she repeats the story, she drives the hurt and anger deeper into her heart and mind.

3. Read Ephesians 4:29.
   (a) What are we *not* to let our talk degenerate into?

   (b) What should our talk do for others?

Don't let anger run unchecked. Don't give the Devil an opportunity to gain a foothold in your life by rehearsing your anger and driving the hurts deeper into your mind and spirit.

We must reverse our anger by redirecting it and refocusing on something else.

4. What should we focus on, according to Ephesians 4:32? Why?

Anger Must Be Controlled

Do you have a temper? Do you control it? Do you (or any of your family members) yell, scream, or slam doors? *Don't sin by letting anger control you.* God wants to help you with this area of weakness. He wants to give you victory over uncontrolled anger.

5. What advice does Psalm 37:8 give us regarding anger?

Proverbs 14:29 deals with the problem of controlling anger. The verse refers to two people with opposite reactions.

6. Based on Proverbs 14:29, summarize what happens in an incident when
   (a) a person is *slow* to become angry.

   (b) a person is *quick* to become angry.

Uncontrolled anger causes people to say things they don't realize or mean. They might say such things as, "I hate you!" or "You're stupid." These kinds of words injure and hurt family and friends, and, though they may be forgiven, they still leave scars.

We can control an angry situation by what we say.

7. According to Proverbs 15:1, 2, and 4, how can our speech stir up anger or downplay it?

According to Proverbs 19:11, a person's discretion (wisdom) causes him or her to defer anger, or to exercise patience. It is the person's "glory" (it is honorable) to "pass over" a transgression.

8. (a) What does it mean to "pass over a transgression"?

(b) Has anyone ever "passed over" one of your transgressions? If so, summarize the event. If not, can you think of a Bible character who "passed over" someone else's transgression?

Venting our anger *does not* make us less angry; it makes us angrier. But controlling anger and patiently overlooking offenses *do* help us become less angry.

9. Proverbs 17:14 likens anger to a reservoir of water that develops a small leak. What does this illustration teach us about anger?

Conquer Anger, or It Will Conquer You

Think of emotional hurts that you know were caused by anger. The people involved could have avoided those hurts if they had allowed the Holy Spirit to dominate their lives.

10. Read Proverbs 19:19.
    (a) What consequence do angry people face?

    (b) What happens when someone tries to help an angry person?

The time between an upsetting situation and our reaction to it is a small window of opportunity in which to choose our course of action.

11. Read Proverbs 29:20. What does God say about the person who speaks before thinking?

12. Proverbs 15:18 talks about two kinds of people.
    (a) Who are these people?

    (b) How does each respond to life?

    You can either conquer your anger by quickly thinking how to handle the situation in a wise fashion (with a brief prayer to God), or you can do what comes naturally: get mad and tell someone off. We could liken this choice to having a fire and two buckets—one filled with water and the other with gasoline. Throw water on the fire, and it's doused. Throw gasoline on it, and it grows. When strife starts, we can throw either water (a patient, calm response) or gasoline (an angry response) on the situation. "Water" will cool it down; "gasoline" will fuel it up. It is a good idea to ask for God's wisdom to help you say what would please Him. *A quick prayer will help you keep your anger under control.*

13. Read Proverbs 22:24 and 25. To keep from becoming angry people, what do we need to avoid?

14. Our Savior set the example for conquering anger. What did He encourage us to be in Matthew 5:9?

Key Actions

People who say they cannot control their anger are kidding themselves. For instance, did you ever hear two people (perhaps one of them was you) in an angry argument, when suddenly the phone rang. One of them answered the phone—using a calm, polite voice. If that person could control her anger when answering the phone, she certainly could have controlled it in the previous conversation.

How do you control your anger? And who taught you to respond this way? Do you take responsibility for your anger, or do you blame it on someone else? No one can make you angry; you have to allow the person to do so.

15. Answer the following two questions.
    (a) What two kinds of people does Proverbs 12:16 mention?

    (b) How do they differ when it comes to anger?

16. Read James 1:19 and 20.
    (a) Based on James 1:19, what three things should we be when we face situations that anger us?

    Be _____ to _____.

    Be _____ to _____.

    Be _____ to _____.

(b) According to James 1:20, why should we *be* these
   things?

Do you recognize unrighteous anger and realize that it dis-
pleases God? Are you experiencing more anger than you had
realized? Are you holding on to your anger, or are you making
sure it is solved by the end of the day (or sooner)?

17. Read Ecclesiastes 7:9. What did Solomon, the wisest man,
    say about hasty anger?

18. Read Romans 12:17–21. How do you think a Christian
    woman would act if she were obeying these verses (espe-
    cially in reference to the revenge side of anger)?

19. Romans 12:19–21 tells us how to handle angry situations.
    What specific counsel does verse 21 give us?

20. How do you see yourself putting Romans 12:19–21 into
    action?

Locking God's Truths into Our Hearts

🔑 *Don't dwell on anger; deal with it.* Has anger ever affected you physically? Most people would have to answer yes. Anger can increase our blood pressure and make our hearts beat faster. How has it affected you? How has it affected someone you know?

🔑 *Seek to experience some solitude; then try to think about the situations you are facing.* Ask God to help you think before you speak in anger when you face a crisis. Ask God to help you control your anger.

🔑 *Don't give the Devil victory by constantly talking about things that anger you and keeping them fresh in your mind.* Reinforcement will make you bitter. Learn to tell your problems to God, not others.

🔑 *List some Scriptures that you can claim to help you face situations that make you angry*—perhaps some that were mentioned in this lesson. Start memorizing some of these verses, and recall them when you are tempted to become angry.

🔑 *Don't be a burden of ungodly emotions to others or grieve the Holy Spirit by being an angry person.* Are you expecting God to help you with the problem of anger? Do you want His help? Don't focus on yourself but on helping others.

🔑 *Let God fight your battles for you.* One of the most encouraging Scriptures on handling anger and letting God deal with people who upset us is 2 Chronicles 20:15.

God told King Jehoshaphat, "Be not afraid nor dismayed by reason of this great multitude; for the battle is not yours, but God's." This is a good Scripture verse to turn to when you are tempted to become angry. The battle is not yours; it is the Lord's.

Take the counsel in Hebrews 10:24 of helping others to grow spiritually. What are some specific ways you could help others?

Burning the Candle at Both Ends

Key Word: Burnout

"Let us not be weary in well doing: for in due season we shall reap, if we faint not" (Galatians 6:9).

A CANDLE BURNING AT both ends may give off twice as much light, but it will also burn twice as fast. Are you burning the candle at both ends? The result is a feeling called burnout. The dictionary defines "burnout" as "exhaustion of physical or emotional strength or motivation, usually as a result of prolonged stress or frustration." It is also a name for "a person suffering from burnout."

Burnout strikes the most productive people (some people aren't active enough to experience burnout). When burnout hits people, they suddenly discover they've lost their strength and find themselves mentally, emotionally, and physically exhausted. Some people say that they would rather *burn out* than *rust out,* but actually neither one is good. Both hinder our service for Christ.

King Solomon is a classic example of burnout. The subject of burnout is woven throughout the book of Ecclesiastes. Solomon amassed more power and wealth than anyone who lived before him. He was able to buy anything he wanted or desired. How would you like to be in that position? Wouldn't you think this kind of lifestyle would bring happiness? It didn't! Eventually Solomon arrived at the place where life seemed futile and empty. For him, work lost its meaning and value. The thrill of life had gone. He felt bored with his extravagant lifestyle. He had the feeling of "been there, done that."

In this lesson we'll study what Solomon observed and concluded about burnout, and, by doing so, we will learn how to avoid burnout.

Unlocking the Truths about Burnout

When work loses its meaning and value, we feel *driven* instead of *called* to do our work. We forget that God will enable us to accomplish the job He has called us to do—not in our own strength, but in His strength (Philippians 4:13; 1 Peter 5:10; 2 Peter 1:3). Ultimately we do not gain satisfaction in our own accomplishments but only in what God accomplishes through us.

Let's look at Solomon's life for some typical signs of burnout.

1. (a) According to Ecclesiastes 2:17, how did Solomon feel about life? about work?

    (b) Why did he feel that way?

Solomon's burnout came from his frustration over life. He found life meaningless in spite of his efforts to find fulfillment in a variety of ways.

Wrong Ways to Relieve Burnout

Solomon set out upon a quest for satisfaction based on the material and the worldly (Ecclesiastes 2).

2. Read Ecclesiastes 2:1.
    (a) What did Solomon try to live for?

    (b) How did it turn out?

Pleasure brings us happiness for a while; then we realize that our inner emptiness is still there.

3. Read Ecclesiastes 2:4–9.
    (a) What did Solomon seek?

    (b) How did this experiment turn out (v. 9)?

Many people believe they will be happy after they achieve a certain goal. Life without God at the center is meaningless no matter what great things we seem to accomplish.

Solomon attained more greatness than anyone had ever achieved. Often we think, "If only I could achieve this or that, then I would be happy." Achievement didn't make Solomon happy! It won't make you happy either!

When these things did not satisfy, Solomon tried yet another tactic.

4. According to the first part of Ecclesiastes 2:10, what did he do?

Solomon could satisfy his every whim. Imagine that! Did getting his heart's desires satisfy Solomon? No. Nothing but God brings long-lasting satisfaction.

Results of Burnout

To have satisfaction and fulfillment in life, we need to do things that have lasting value. Even though Solomon had great wisdom, he missed this important fact.

5. Read Ecclesiastes 2:11. How did Solomon view his life's activities?

6. How does Mark 8:36 summarize this important lesson that Solomon sadly missed?

This verse should be a warning to anyone who has not accepted Christ—a warning against the folly of "this world only" thinking. Instead, we should concentrate on these important questions: What is my relationship with God? Where will I spend eternity? and How does God want me to live?

7. Read Psalm 16:11. By knowing God and living for Him, what can we have now and later?

Key Actions

The book of Ecclesiastes has some suggestions to help us overcome burnout, or better yet, to protect us from it. Try the following suggestions: manage your time well, control your mouth, keep your commitments to God, maintain a close and intimate relationship with your mate, do your work with excellence and vigor, help others succeed, practice an attitude of gratitude toward God, and maintain a close and faithful walk with God.

⇨ *Manage your time well.* Burnouts abuse time with overloads and imbalance.

8. What does Ecclesiastes 3:1 teach us about managing the times and seasons of our lives?

Everyone has the same amount of time—168 hours a week. No one can do everything, so we have to balance our use of time.

9. (a) List the priorities of your life.

   (b) How well are you balancing the time you spend on these priorities? (Check the statement that applies best.)

__ Not very well. I need to get _____ back into balance.

__ Fairly well. I get by okay. But I could improve in the area of _____.

__ Well. I have learned to balance all aspects of my life, as long as nothing new is added.

__ Very well. Balancing my time is well under control. I should be mentoring others in how to balance their time.

⇨ *Control your mouth.* Burnouts often say critical, complaining things that hurt the cause of God, their families, and friends.

10. What does Ecclesiastes 5:2 say about controlling what we say?

Burnouts are often miserable people who find great satisfaction in making other people miserable. Don't be a complainer, and beware of keeping company with complaining people.

⇨ *Keep your commitments to God.* Obedience to God keeps us on track in every area. It keeps us from depending on our feelings, and it helps us focus on our commitments.

11. What does Ecclesiastes 5:4 say about keeping our commitments to God?

An important principle for life is that we do not *feel* our way out of a bad attitude; we *work* our way out of it. Our feelings can change, but our commitment to God should not change.

⇨ *Maintain a close, intimate relationship with your mate.* If you are not married, you should have a solid friend or relative with whom you can share your feelings.

12. In light of Ecclesiastes 9:9, what should characterize your relationship with your mate?

Spend quality time together. Learn to have fun together regardless of your age. It is important for a married couple to have fun times together without always having the children or another married couple with them. Having one's mate as one's best friend adds spice to life and helps keep a couple on course. Do not assume that a good Christian couple automatically has a successful or good marriage. All marriage relationships require maintenance. They require constant work!

⇨ *Do your work with excellence and vigor.* A job well done results in a sense of satisfaction. It should include joy as well.

13. How do Ecclesiastes 9:10 and Colossians 3:23 emphasize that we should do our work with excellence and vigor?

Christians have a special job that will invigorate their lives: the work of sharing the gospel with others. Nothing can substitute for the joy of soul winning.

As we think of our God-given work here on earth, it is important to have some goals and projects. Take the example of how God made trees. No tree is ever fully grown. If a tree is alive, it is growing. When it stops growing, it will die. We should always be growing spiritually and mentally.

⇨ *Help others succeed.* When you are willing to help others, God will undertake for you in a special way. Burnouts become self-oriented. Taking our eyes off ourselves and onto the needs of others will do wonders for us.

One great man said, "The measure of a man is not how many servants he has, but how many he serves." If you will learn how to help others reach their goals, you will be helping yourself reach yours; but if you do evil to others, evil will come back to you.

⇨ *Practice an attitude of gratitude to God.* Being grateful for God's blessings not only pleases God, but it also does us a lot of good.

14. According to Ecclesiastes 5:19 (especially the last statement of the verse), what should we call all the wonderful things God has done for us?

We need to praise God for His blessings because praise lifts our burdens and puts things into perspective. Deuteronomy 26:11 says, "And thou shalt rejoice in every good thing which the

LORD thy God hath given unto thee, and unto thine house." And Nehemiah 8:10 states, "The joy of the LORD is your strength."

⇨ *Maintain a close, faithful walk with God.* Even though this suggestion is the last one, it is not least. Actually, it is the most important point of all. We must maintain a close, faithful walk with God.

15. (a) What does Ecclesiastes 12:1 tell us to remember?

   (b) If we do not heed Ecclesiastes 12:1, what will happen in the latter days of our lives?

Locking God's Truths into Our Hearts

🔑 *Evaluate yourself.* Are you going through the motions of living to the fullest or just trying to survive? Does life seem empty and meaningless to you? Or do you carry out your work with vigor and excellence?

🔑 *Identify your focus.* What have you done to achieve purpose and fulfillment in life? Are you completely focused on yourself, or do you try to help others? Who could you help this week? How?

🔑 *Learn to manage your time well.* How would you sum up the activities of your life? Do you manage your time well? How could you do better?

🔑 *Keep your conversations with others positive and pleasing to God.* Do you praise and thank Him for the blessings

He has brought your way?

O—🔑 *If you are married, keep a close relationship with your mate.* Are you willing to take the initiative to make your marriage better? There is always room for improvement, no matter how long you have been married or how great your marriage has been.

O—🔑 *Be rightly related to Jesus Christ.* Do you know Christ as your Savior? If not, see Romans 10:9 and 13, Acts 16:31, and John 1:12. If you are a born-again believer in Jesus Christ, do you have a close walk with Him? Colossians 2:6 says, "As ye have therefore received Christ Jesus the Lord, so walk ye in him." What could you do to improve your spiritual life?

O—🔑 *Remember, it is best to begin to work on avoiding burnout immediately; don't wait!*

O—🔑 *Fear God.* A final key for burnout is found in Ecclesiastes 12:13: "Let us hear the conclusion of the whole matter: Fear God, and keep his commandments: for this is the whole duty of man."

O—🔑 *Recognize what's truly important.* Our lesson from Solomon tells us that all the things we have accomplished for life here and now will one day disappear and become meaningless. Only what we have done for Christ will last for eternity.

Lord, Help Me Change

Key Word: Change

"Therefore if any man be in Christ, he is a new creature: old things are passed away; behold, all things are become new" (2 Corinthians 5:17).

DO YOU EVER wish you could start over? Probably all of us would answer yes to this question. Most of us wish for another chance in some area of our lives. Maybe we wouldn't have done things *differently* as much as we would have done *more* or *less.* But the truth is that we can't go back and relive our lives. We can, however, learn to change in the future by learning from the past.

Life is like a fiber optic decoration—always changing. Change adds color and variety to our lives and keeps them from becoming boring and mundane. And most people think they need to change something (e.g., their weight, intelligence, health, or wealth), but few are willing to do what it takes to make the change.

Some things in life we *can't change,* but most people don't

31

change what they *can change.* Life will make more sense when we understand that God wants to change us. What may seem to be a crisis or difficulty may really be an opportunity for God to change us and make us more like His Son.

Let's look at some ways God changes us. Ask yourself, *How is God trying to change me?*

Unlocking the Truths about Change

Here are seven truths to consider about change.

⇨ God has a plan for your life.

⇨ God will help you know what His plan is.

⇨ God wants you to fulfill this plan.

⇨ God will help you complete His plan for you.

⇨ You can experience God's blessing by carrying out His plan.

⇨ You must change to grow into the plan God has for you.

⇨ When you grow, your family, friends, and coworkers will benefit.

The right change can make an incredible difference in our lives! The wrong change only redoubles our efforts on things that won't work. The wrong change only destroys.

The most important change is the one that occurs when someone becomes a child of God.

1. Read 1 John 5:12 and 13.
   (a) What change takes place when a person receives God's Son (v. 12)?

   (b) Can you be sure you have this eternal life that changes a person and causes her to live forever (v. 13)?

2. According to 2 Corinthians 5:17, what change takes place when we receive this new life? (The word "creature" means "creation.")

Everything in our past can be just that: in our past. And everything from now on can be new: brand-new in Christ, that is—changed.

A dramatic change takes place at the start of the Christian life.

3. Read Ephesians 5:8 and 9.
    (a) What words contrast a person's life before and after the change of salvation (v. 8)?

    (b) How are we to respond to this change?

Change not only marks the beginning of the Christian life, but it also characterizes the process that takes place as we grow in Christ.

4. What are some negative and positive changes that should occur, according to 1 Peter 2:1–3?

We live in a changing world with changing people. God is the only One Who does not change.

5. Read Numbers 23:19 and Hebrews 13:8.

   (a) What comforting fact does Numbers 23:19 tell us about God?

   (b) What does Hebrews 13:8 tell us about His Son?

In an insecure, changing world, we can find security in an unchanging God and His Son, Jesus Christ.

Crisis Causes Change

Often when God wants to change us, He puts us through a crisis. Few people change in times of prosperity and peace. Most people need a reason to change. One person has said that "adversity is the window of opportunity for change."

God used crises in the life of Jacob to help him understand his need of change. He had several crises in his early adulthood. First, he "bought" the birthright instead of waiting for it (Genesis 25:29–34). Verse 23 records God's saying that the second-born, Jacob, would be the heir. Then Jacob tricked his father into giving him the blessing that should have been his anyway (27:1–29). The blessing, along with the birthright, belonged to the heir. Jacob forced the issue through trickery. As a result, Esau hated Jacob and threatened to kill him as soon as their father was dead (27:41).

6. "Jacob" means "one who follows on another's heels; supplanter." "Supplanted" means "superseded (another) especially by force or treachery." According to Genesis 27:36, why did Esau think Jacob was rightly named?

Even after Jacob left home (Genesis 28:1–5), he faced crises. Jacob's father-in-law, Laban, changed Jacob's wages ten times (31:7) and tricked Jacob by marrying him to Leah even though he had worked for Rachel (29:14–30).

Jacob was familiar with conniving, tricking, and taking advantage of people, so he continued trying to out-deceive Laban through a deal he made with Laban. Jacob asked for his own flock, and Laban agreed to let him have the speckled and spotted cattle and goats as well as the brown sheep (Genesis 30:29–43). But Laban deceived and cheated Jacob (vv. 35, 36). He quickly took the female animals that he had promised to Jacob and sent them away with his sons so it would be difficult for Jacob to get them back. Jacob had a plan too: he peeled the bark from branches and placed them in the watering troughs, superstitiously thinking they would cause the animals to reproduce (vv. 37–43). Although Jacob was trying to trick Laban, God Himself was responsible for the growth of Jacob's flocks (31:7–12).

7. (a) In your opinion what are some reasons people resist changing for the better?

   (b) What are some obstacles that keep you personally from changing for the better?

After any of his crises, Jacob could have changed his life and started living right. But he didn't. It is our natural tendency to resist change, especially if we think the cost of change is too high.

In the meantime, God was working in Jacob's life. He did not intend for Jacob to stay with Laban. Genesis 31:3 says that "the LORD said unto Jacob, Return unto the land of thy fathers, and to thy kindred; and I will be with thee." After twenty years it was time for Jacob to start back home. A reading of Genesis 31:1–6 shows that several people wanted Jacob to leave Laban: Laban's sons (v. 1), Laban (v. 2), the Lord (v. 3), and Rachel and Leah (vv. 14–16).

Going home was frightening for Jacob; he appeared to be quite nervous as he approached his brother, who had said, "I'm going to kill Jacob!" (Genesis 27:41).

Genesis 32:1–7 records that Jacob sent servants ahead as scouts. They came back with the report that Esau had four hundred men with him (v. 6). Jacob then devised a plan to divide the group into two. If the first group was attacked, the second group could escape. Then Jacob prayed, reminding God of His command to return and His promise to take care of Jacob (v. 9). Jacob approached God with humility (v. 10). He told God that he didn't deserve God's mercies. Jacob was not trusting in his own manipulation and deceit to deliver him from Esau's anger (vv. 11, 12). He asked God to deliver him so he could protect his family. He reminded God of His promise to give him innumerable descendants.

Although Jacob humbly prayed to God, he did what he could to appease Esau and to save himself and his loved ones. Genesis 32:13–23 explains the details of Jacob's plan. First, he would give Esau two hundred female goats, twenty male goats, two hundred ewes, twenty rams, thirty female camels and their colts, forty cows, ten bulls, twenty female donkeys, and ten foals. His servants would tell Esau, "These are presents from your brother Jacob to you." Jacob would protect himself and his family by keeping them at the back and appeasing

Esau before he got to them. Then he sent the groups across the brook ahead of him.

8. Read Genesis 32:24–26. Summarize what happened after Jacob's possessions and family left him and he was alone.

9. According to Genesis 32:30, with Whom did Jacob wrestle?

10. Read Genesis 32:27–31. The Man Whom Jacob wrestled with changed two things about Jacob.
    (a) What did the Man change about Jacob (v. 28)?

    (b) How did He change Jacob physically (v. 31)?

Big Problem: Who Is in Control?

Jacob's biggest battle was not with his brother or even with his father-in-law; it was with God. The biggest battle you face is not a struggle for control with some great problem or person but with the Almighty. Let's look at what is involved in giving God control of our lives.

Read 1 Samuel 15:22 and 23. Here was another man who had problems obeying God.

11. (a) According to verse 22, what did Samuel tell Saul is more important than sacrifice?

    (b) How did Samuel view Saul's disobedience?

Too often we want our own way, not God's way. Obedience is more important to God than sacrifice.

12. Read Proverbs 3:5 and 6. How can we give God control of our lives?

13. What does Proverbs 3:6 say will happen to those who are committed to God?

God wants our commitment, trust, and obedience. He wants us to seek Him and to "not let [Him] go" until we make the changes He wants in our lives. God wants us to discover whether we mean business.

Usually we pray for God to get us out of a crisis. That's okay. But we also need to ask God to change us through the crisis to make us what He wants us to be. Jacob knew the Person he wrestled with could change him. He can change you too.

Commitment to Change

The *Bible Knowledge Commentary: Old Testament* makes these observations about Jacob's struggle with the Man:

The fact that the match lasted **till daybreak** is significant. For the darkness symbolized Jacob's situation. Fear and uncertainty seized him. If Jacob had perceived that he was to fight God, he would never have engaged in the fight, let alone have continued all night.

On the other hand the fact that the wrestling lasted till daybreak suggests a long, decisive bout. In fact the Assailant did not defeat **Jacob** till He resorted to something extraordinary.

At last the Assailant **touched** Jacob **so that his hip** went out of joint. The point is clear: the Assailant gave Himself the advantage. Jacob, the deceitful fighter, was crippled by a supernatural blow. In a word, like so many of his rivals, Jacob now encountered Someone he could not defeat. (John F. Walvoord and Roy B. Zuck, eds. [Colorado Springs: Victor Books, 1985], 81.)

14. Reread Genesis 32:24–31. What did Jacob say he had to have before he would give up wrestling with the Man?

Though crippled and unable to win, **Jacob** clung to his Assailant for a blessing. Then both the identity of the Assailant and the significance of the fight dawned on Jacob. Once he realized who his Assailant was (v. 28) **Jacob** held on resolutely, pleading for a blessing. It is significant that in response to Jacob's request for a blessing **the Man asked . . . What is your name?** When one remembers that in the Old Testament one's name is linked to his nature, the point becomes clear: Jacob's pattern of life had to be radically changed! In saying his name, **Jacob** had to reveal his whole nature. Here the "heel-catcher" was caught, and had to confess his true nature before he could be **blessed.** *(The Bible Knowledge Commentary: Old Testament,* 81.)

15. (a) Could God have overpowered Jacob?

(b) Why do you think He chose not to?

(c) What lesson from God to you do you find in this Bible account?

The Man could have eliminated Jacob; He could have turned him into dust. But He didn't. He wanted Jacob to learn what only a struggle could teach him. Commitment to God requires us to humble ourselves before God through a crisis or through a struggle with Him. When we are humbled, we ask for God's blessing.

16. What are some of the things you have learned when you have wrestled with God about a certain crisis in your life?

If God immediately gave us everything we asked for, we would become "spoiled brats." Don't you appreciate the things you have to struggle for more than what comes easily? God wants to help us develop character more than He wants us to be comfortable. Persistence helps develop character in us.

17. Read 1 Corinthians 15:58.
   (a) What does this verse command us about persistence in the Christian life?

   (b) What happens to our persistent labor for God?

Key Actions

Are you facing a personal crisis? If so, perhaps God wants to make a change in your life. Adversity is one of the main reasons for change. (Someone has said, "If we don't change when we see the light, we'll change when we feel the heat.") Few people change when they are in prosperity and peace. They don't say, "I have a great life right now, so I think I'll make some changes." Usually they wait until life is difficult and then say, "Something in my life has got to change." Change begins with you.

18. Take inventory of your life. How have you changed for the better? How do you still need to change?

Remember God often uses crises to bring us to Himself. The biggest struggle you have right now is not your health, finances, or relationship with someone. *The biggest struggle you have right now is over who has control of your life.* A crisis can be defined as a struggle with God. Why? Because we want to continue in our sin and have our own way. David gave some good counsel on this subject in Psalm 32:5.

19. Read Psalm 32:5.
    (a) What should you do first to start change in your life?

    (b) What will God do?

We rarely change until the pain we feel from the problem exceeds the pain we fear from change. Although Jacob did not realize it when he began to struggle with the Man, there was no way for Jacob to win. Sometimes, like Jacob, we wrestle in a no-win situation. Is God trying to get your attention with a no-win situation?

20. According to Luke 11:28, where should you turn and what should be your resource when you encounter a no-win situation?

God can't change you until you openly admit your sin. Your confession won't surprise God; He knows your sin. So stop blaming others and admit your sin to Him. Telling God, "I'm the problem" is a breakthrough. Watch out for pride! God gives grace to the humble. He also gives them the power to change. God can take your weaknesses and make them your strengths.

Locking God's Truths into Our Hearts

🔑 *As a believer, you have a new name.* God gave Jacob a new name, a new identity. Jacob's name meant "supplanter." Jacob lived up to his name. But God changed his name from Jacob ("supplanter" or "grabber") to Israel ("prince with God" or "God fights"). God can do the same for you. What was your former "name"? What is your "name" now?

🔑 *Seek God's blessing.* Jacob was serious about getting God's blessing. What does God's blessing mean to you? Are you seriously seeking God's blessing?

🔑 *Appreciate your "reminder."* God gave Jacob a reminder of this experience—he limped the rest of his life. God gives us various reminders of our struggles with Him. What are some of your reminders, or, if you don't have any, what are someone else's reminders? (These reminders may not be physical. They could be visual or mental; for example, a certain sight reminds you of the struggle.)

🔑 *Recognize that "when [we are] weak, then [are we] strong" (2 Corinthians 12:10).* After we meet with God, we never walk the same; our lives change. Jacob's limp reminded him of his experience with God. Jacob probably never ran again. His hip caused him trouble. God touched Jacob's joint of strength and created weakness. God does His deepest work in our lives when He changes our identity. This new identity changes the way we see ourselves.

🔑 *Evaluate your relationship with God.* Here are three questions for you: (1) Will I obey God? (2) Will I trust God? (3) Am I committed to do God's will for my life? Your biggest problem is simply this: Am I going to obey and trust God, and am I committed to do His will for my life?

🔑 *Yield control to God.* The root of all our problems is our desire to control and decide for ourselves. We want to be our own gods. And that is why God wrestles with us—because He wants to control us. All our lives we try to take control instead of letting Him have control. What area in your life are you struggling to control? Turn it over to God.

🔑 *Admit to God when you are in a no-win situation, and ask for His help.* In Genesis 32 Jacob couldn't overpower God. Jacob could not win. Are you in a no-win situation? What are you going to do about it?

View a difficult situation as an opportunity, not a reason for self-pity. Are you facing a difficult situation? Instead of feeling sorry for yourself and seeking sympathy from others, try to look at the difficulty in a different way. Could this situation cause you to deepen your relationship with God? Do you think God allowed it to happen for a certain purpose? Seek God's help. Yield to God's will and purpose for your life. Realize that the battle is not yours, but God's.

Believing the Unbelievable

Key Word: Faith

"Whosoever shall say unto this mountain, Be thou removed, and be thou cast into the sea; and shall not doubt in his heart, but shall believe that those things which he saith shall come to pass; he shall have whatsoever he saith" (Mark 11:23).

F AITH" IS A small word that makes a big difference in a Christian's life. We are saved by faith in Jesus Christ. Our Christian life is a walk of faith. Have you by faith received Christ as your Savior? Some believers never move much beyond salvation. But for the Christian who wants to live by faith, there is more.

Has God worked in your life in such a way that you know beyond a shadow of a doubt that He has done it? Are you proceeding in life with confidence and expectation that God will bring greater things to pass? Our God specializes in working through ordinary people who believe in God's extraordinary power to do His work through them. Will you pray that God will increase your ministry for Him? Then trust God for the resources, people, and strength to do His work.

Do you want your life to make a mark for God? If so, pause for a moment and ask yourself, *What's the "mountain" in my life?* Putting your faith in God to remove your "mountain" can change your whole life.

I trust that this lesson will open your life to the mighty working of God's power.

Unlocking the Truths about Faith

1. Read Mark 11:22.
   (a) What is the difference between a command and a suggestion?

   (b) What command (not suggestion) did Jesus give in Mark 11:22?

Why do we give commands? For instance, how often do you need to command a child to eat dessert? We command people to do something that does not come naturally. Jesus knew we needed to be commanded to "have faith in God." He knew that having faith in God would not come easy for us.

2. Read Mark 11:23. What is the key to removing "mountains" (problems) in your life?

The phrase in Mark 11:24 "believe that ye receive them" actually means "believe you have received them." Understanding this meaning sheds a whole new light on the verse.

3. With this truth in mind, what does Mark 11:24 teach us about faith in God?

God defined faith in Hebrews 11:1: "Faith is the substance of things hoped for, the evidence of things not seen." Let's look at this definition in more detail.

4. Read Hebrews 11:1.
   (a) The word "substance" means "being sure of." As you consider the definition of "substance" in Hebrews 11:1, what is one characteristic of faith?

   (b) The word "evidence" has the meaning of "certain of." As you consider the definition of "evidence" in Hebrews 11:1, what is faith certain of?

A homemade definition of faith is this: Everything is not okay, but that's okay because everything is going to be okay. Faith makes us sure of what we hope for and certain of what we cannot see. Occasionally we hear people say, "Oh, just have faith!" But having faith will do no good if we do not have faith in the right object. We must place our faith in God.

There are no limitations when we are trusting God. Biblical faith is based upon the person and promises of God. Our "certainty" must be anchored in God. Remember, Mark 11:22 does not read, "Have faith," but rather "Have faith in God." When it comes to providing the desired end, or goal, faith is no better than the object of its trust. Sometimes people talk about having faith in themselves, but that is a faulty source because of our human limitations. The only faith that counts is the kind that makes us sure of what we hope for and certain of what we do not see. This kind of faith can be found only in God.

Let's look at a Biblical example of faith. Mary the mother of our Savior had this kind of faith. Luke 1:26–38 recounts the angel's message to Mary that she would be the mother of the Messiah. Notice that the angel did not tell Mary that she was pregnant with the Messiah, but that she would become pregnant and give birth to the Messiah. Mary couldn't figure out how such a thing could be, since she was a virgin. But the angel told her that the Holy Spirit would come upon her and that God would be the father of her child.

5. The statement by the angel in Luke 1:37 reveals another aspect of faith. What is the implication for us?

Are you facing a humanly impossible situation? Ask God for faith and believe Him for the impossible. Mary showed her faith by yielding to God's plan for her, and she believed that He would accomplish what He had said (Luke 1:38). Faith in God for the impossible involves complete submission to the will of God.

Doubt and Do Without

Many common problems in the lives of Christians reveal a lack of faith. Let's look at three categories of "doubt and do without."

First, worry is a common problem for many Christians. But

worry evidences a lack of faith in God. Trust is the opposite of worry. Trust prevents us from worrying.

   6. Read Jeremiah 17:7 and 8.
     (a) How did God describe those who trust Him?

     (b) What would rob us of these blessings?

     The difference between worry and trust can be compared to the difference between a parched dwarf juniper tree in the desert and a flourishing fruit tree drawing sustenance from a peaceful river. Basically, worry is an insult to God's love and to His ability to handle our problems.

Second, guilt is another result connected to a lack of faith in God. When a Christian woman harbors guilt after confessing sin to God, she is showing a lack of faith in God's forgiveness.

   7. What does Psalm 32:5 teach us about forgiveness?

     It is by faith that we accept God's forgiveness of our sins, regardless of feelings such as guilt.

Third, disobedience also stems from a lack of faith in God.

   8. Read Luke 6:46.
     (a) What rebuke did Jesus give to His disciples?

(b) If we really believe that Christ is Lord of our lives, what should follow?

Believe and Receive

Now let's look at what happens when we "believe and receive."

First, believing opens the door of salvation.

9. Read Ephesians 2:8 and 9. What part does faith play in our salvation?

Salvation takes place when we make a personal decision to place our faith in Jesus Christ's sacrificial death on the cross to pay for our sins and in God's acceptance of Jesus' sacrifice, as seen in His glorious resurrection.

Second, the degree to which we claim God's promises sets the level of blessing in our lives.

10. How do you see this relationship between claiming God's promises and the degree of blessing in the healing of the blind men in Matthew 9:27–30?

Just as the blind men were drastically changed because of their faith, our lives can be drastically changed by our faith in God to solve the problems of our lives (that is, to remove our "mountains"). Jesus was more concerned about the men's faith in Him than in their need to see. He was more concerned about their spiritual well-being than about their physical plight.

Another illustration of the importance of not limiting God's blessing through unbelief is found in 2 Kings 4:1–7.

11. Read 2 Kings 4:1–7, and answer the following questions.
    (a) What crisis did the widow face (v. 1)?

    (b) Where did she go for help (v. 1)?

    (c) What did the prophet tell her to do (vv. 3, 4)?

    (d) How did her faith affect her future?

What an account of how faith makes a difference in our lives! May God help us remember that our faith in God and obedience to His Word affect our future. So many times we go through life simply trying to survive rather than seeking God's direction and help for abundant blessings.

Great Faith vs. Little Faith

As far as I can tell, the majority of Christian people today do not practice great faith. Seeing examples of faith in the Scriptures helps us understand great faith. We will look at both ends of the "faith spectrum." On one side is what Christ cited as "great faith." On the other side is what He called "little faith."

Great Faith. Read the account of the Roman centurion in Matthew 8:5–10 and 13.

12. What was unique about the centurion's faith (v. 10)?

Notice how the centurion went to Jesus pleading for help. He had a humble faith. He also had an unquestioning confident faith in the authority and power of Christ and His word. As a result, Christ honored and blessed the centurion's faith and healed his servant immediately.

Another time that Christ cited "great faith" was in the case of a Canaanite woman (Matthew 15:21–28). She approached Jesus humbly and persistently. She came to Him "crying," which shows the burden on her heart.

She also came with a submissive attitude. She didn't demand; she pleaded. And she referred to Jesus as "Lord" and "Son of David." She requested that He heal her daughter who was demon-possessed.

At first Jesus ignored her (v. 23). He responded as if He didn't care about her (vv. 24, 26). But He wanted to teach His disciples a lesson. They were prejudiced against the woman because of her nationality. The woman did not let Jesus' response discourage her, even when Jesus told her that He had come only to Israel. She kept on pleading with Him for help.

After He got His disciples' attention, Jesus healed the woman's daughter and said that the woman had "great" faith (v. 28).

There is a lesson here for all of us: Though we cannot always understand God's seeming silence or slowness to respond to our needs, we can be confident of Christ's loving interest and by faith trust Him for our needs.

Little Faith. Having looked at one end of the "faith spectrum," where Christ honored "great faith," let's look at four cases in which Christ rebuked "little faith."

➪ *Worry.* Read the account of Mary and Martha in Luke 10:38–42.

13. Why did Jesus rebuke Martha and commend Mary (vv. 41, 42)?

Worries about the cares of life hinder our relationship with God.

➪ *Fear.* Another time Jesus rebuked "little faith" is found in Matthew 8:23–27. Read these verses.

14. According to Matthew 8:26, what basic problem did the disciples have?

Notice that before Jesus calmed the storm, He rebuked the disciples for their lack of faith. The disciples should have thought, *This ship can't sink with Christ on board.*

Jesus is always present in the storms of life, even though sometimes His presence is more evident than at other times.

➪ *Doubt.* During another storm, recorded in Matthew 14:24–33, Christ walked out to the disciples' storm-tossed ship. Eleven of the disciples stayed in the boat and watched; only one got out. Faith takes a step into the unknown. If you want to walk on water, you have to get out of the boat!

15. Read Matthew 14:31. What was the reason for "little faith"?

Like so many of us, Peter took his eyes off Christ (v. 30) and his focus off Christ's word (v. 29). But don't be too hard on Peter.

After all, he was the only one who got out of the boat.

At first, Peter watched Jesus. Then Peter focused on himself and his circumstances. As he focused on himself, Peter may have thought, *I've fished this lake for a long time, and nobody—absolutely nobody—has walked on water!* Perhaps, at the same time, Thomas yelled out, "Hey, Pete, watch out for that BIG wave." How often we think just like Peter! But Christ teaches us that faith looks beyond one's self and circumstances. It looks to God.

⇨ *Human reasoning.* A fourth rebuke of "little faith" is found in Matthew 16:6–8.

16. What hindered the disciples' faith (Matthew 16:8)?

The disciples had the problem of human reasoning. Have you ever experienced lack of faith because of human reasoning—you never knew such a thing to happen, so you reasoned that it wouldn't/couldn't happen?

As you review these four examples of "little faith," notice the cycle they followed.

Key Actions

Let's dissect Hebrews 12:1 and 2 to find some ways to build and develop faith. Ask God to increase your faith today.

The word "therefore" in Hebrews 12:1 transitions between chapters 11 and 12. The people mentioned in chapter 11 are known for their faith, and some of them even died for it. These generations of seasoned disciples traveled the road ahead of us. Hebrews 12:1 calls them "a cloud of witnesses."

17. Read Hebrews 12:1. What are some ways these people of "great faith" should motivate us and strengthen our faith?

Sin is excess baggage, so we should throw off all known sin. Some Bible students believe that the phrase "the sin which doth so easily beset [entangle] us" refers to unbelief.

18. According to Hebrews 12:1, how can we get some spiritual exercise?

Our faith will grow as we continue to exercise it in the race of life. Faith, like physical exercise, increases as we use it.

19. Read Hebrews 12:2. Where should our focus be so that our faith will grow?

The words "looking unto Jesus" are better translated "fixing our eyes on Jesus." The Greek word "look" means "to look away from all else," which includes ourselves and our circumstances.

Locking God's Truths into Our Hearts

From a practical application standpoint, let's make some suggestions to develop our walk of faith with God. Here are some ideas on how to claim and act on God's promises.

○━🔑 *Remember times when God answered your prayers and honored your steps of faith.* It is important to record answers to prayers as a reminder of what God has done for you in the past. Use the list to encourage and increase your faith.

○━🔑 *Move forward in your walk of faith by looking for opportunities in your daily life to claim God's promises and act in faith.* Biblical faith is proactive.

○━🔑 *Associate with people who encourage and strengthen your faith.*

○━🔑 *Search out the promises of God that will encourage you to have more faith.* Study the Bible daily, noting Bible promises and examples of faith. Claim these promises and act on them in faith.

○━🔑 *Choose an area of life where you need to trust God in faith; then start trusting Him.* Think big—ask the all-powerful God for big blessings (Ephesians 3:20).

○━🔑 *If needed, take the first step of faith by accepting Christ as your Savior.* Don't delay. Take this step immediately!

God has a great future for you, His child. He has many unclaimed blessings that can be yours for the asking. Your Heavenly Father longs to give you more blessings than you have ever thought to ask for. Remember, you can't walk on water if you don't get out of the boat!

Forgive and Be Forgiven

Key Word: Forgiveness

"Be ye kind one to another, tenderhearted, forgiving one another, even as God for Christ's sake hath forgiven you" (Ephesians 4:32).

WHEN YOU hear the word "forgive," does one particular situation immediately come to your mind? Has someone wronged or mistreated you, and you need to forgive that person? Do you have difficulty speaking well of a certain person? Does the thought of that person make you cringe? We all need to forgive (and be forgiven) at one time or another. Disastrous effects will come upon us if we don't forgive. Forgiving others can be a valuable gift to ourselves. The act of forgiving has huge emotional and physical benefits.

Forgiveness has two sides: the divine and the human. For us to forgive others, it is important to understand God's divine forgiveness. The Bible tells us of the great, mighty, powerful, holy, and just God Who created people who rebel against Him.

It tells of His loving and merciful efforts to bring sinners into fellowship with Him.

Unlocking the Truths about Forgiveness

We read about forgiveness, talk about forgiveness, and hear sermons about forgiveness. We know about God's forgiveness, but do we truly know how to forgive? Let's look at what the Bible teaches about forgiveness.

1. Read Genesis 3:1–24.
   (a) Why did Adam and Eve sin (vv. 1–6)?

   (b) How did they feel after they had sinned (vv. 7–13)?

   (c) What was the result of their sin (vv. 16–19, 23, 24)?

2. Read Romans 3:23. Why does everyone need God's forgiveness?

The need for forgiveness is universal because we have all sinned against God.

3. (a) Why is forgiveness a necessary part of life?

(b) What emotions and feelings develop when a person is wronged or offended?

(c) We know that we all do wrong and hurt or offend others (or get hurt ourselves, even if we know that the offense was unintentional). To restore a previous relationship, what must take place?

We are to model our forgiveness after our Savior's forgiveness.

4. In Luke 23:34 what lesson did Jesus teach us about forgiveness while He was dying on the cross?

Sometimes we need to forgive people who will never ask our forgiveness. Christ did that on the cross when He said, "Father, forgive them; for they know not what they do."

Why We Need to Forgive

Read the prayer Jesus taught His disciples (often called "The Lord's Prayer") in Matthew 6:9–13. The word "debts" (v. 12) has the meaning of "fault," of "something owed." The word "debtors" refers to those who sin against us. According to this prayer, if we are to enjoy fellowship with God, we must practice forgiving others. Our forgiveness of others does not earn God's forgiveness but reflects His forgiveness of us (see Ephesians 4:32). Matthew 6:12 refers to personal fellowship with God (not salvation from sin). A Christian cannot walk in fellowship with God if he or she refuses to forgive others. God expects those who have experienced His forgiveness to forgive others just as He has forgiven them.

Forgiving improves intimate relationships. But those who are reluctant to forgive hurt their relationships with those they love. Forgiving helps us view our loved ones in a Biblical light.

An unforgiving spirit is sin (sometimes called "iniquity" in the Bible).

5. Read Psalm 66:18. What does God say will block our prayers?

We pray, "God, please [do this, give me that, etc.], and God says, "Your iniquity is breaking our fellowship. You need to forgive _____ before I will 'hear' you."

As we think of our need to be forgiven by God and of our need to forgive others, let's look at eight principles stated or suggested in the Scriptures.

⇨ We all sin against God.
⇨ We all continue to sin after salvation.
⇨ We all sin against each other at times.
⇨ Others will sin against us.
⇨ We all need to be forgiven.
⇨ We all need to forgive others.
⇨ People who owe us apologies and restitution may not pay.
⇨ We will be repeatedly wronged by others, "debtors" (plural).

Understanding these principles will help us develop a forgiving spirit toward others.

The Meaning of Forgiveness

To understand what something is, it is often good to define what it is *not.*

Forgiveness does *not* mean, "It didn't matter."

Forgiveness does *not* mean, "Well, I'll get over it."

Forgiveness does *not* mean, "You can treat me any way you wish with no penalty."

Forgiveness does *not* mean, "I'm just going to try to forget it."

Forgiveness is *not* excusing or merely understanding why the wrong was committed.

Forgiveness is *not* revenge.

Forgiveness is *not* assurance that it will never happen again.

Remember: Our forgiveness of others should be like God's forgiveness of us. His forgiveness is unconditional. What is forgiveness for us? *Forgiveness for us is giving up the right to be upset with the offender and losing the desire to strike back.*

According to what you have learned so far in this lesson, would you say people should forgive because *they feel like forgiving* or because *they know that forgiving is the right thing to do?*

6. Would you say forgiveness is a *feeling* or an *action?* Explain your answer.

Forgiveness is a decision of the will. Forgiveness says, "I will not bring this up to you again." Forgiveness is a threefold promise that says,

I will *not* remind you of this affront;

I will *not* report this offense to others;
I will *not* review this wrong over and over to myself.

7. Think through these questions about forgiveness.
   (a) How does *not* bringing up the offense to the offender help us forgive?

   (b) How does *not* talking about the offense help us forgive?

   (c) How does *not* mulling it over and over in our minds help us forgive?

Here are three rules that promote forgiveness:
Rule 1   Give up rigid rules of how you think others should act and talk.
Rule 2   Look at the hurtful incident through the eyes of the other person. Try to see his or her point of view, or at least a neutral viewpoint.
Rule 3   Move twice. First, *move away* from blaming others to accepting them, and then *move on.*

8. Look at each of these rules again. How can each one help a Christian better practice forgiveness?
   Rule 1

Rule 2

Rule 3

Some people do not want to forgive. They think forgiveness will diminish them in some way. They are afraid that if they forgive, people will think they are weak. Others enjoy the attention and consolation they get from being mistreated. Some want the person who wronged them to be punished and to hurt as they do. These attitudes have no place in the Christian's life.

The basis for a forgiving spirit is the reality of Christ's forgiveness of our sins.

9. Read Colossians 3:13. When and why are we to forgive?

God's grace to us moves us to forgive others. Remember that our sins nailed Christ to the cross—and He forgave us.

The Cost of Forgiveness

Remember the Lord's model prayer in Matthew 6:12: "Forgive us our debts, as we forgive our debtors"?

10. If you forgive a debtor who owes you $1,000, how much does it cost you? (This is not a trick question.)

Look at the table below. Forgiveness is costly, not only financially but also emotionally. When we forgive, we have to give up the items in column 1 below. Even though all the items in column 1 are ungodly, sometimes we still like to hold on to them.

11. Draw a line from each characteristic in column 1 to the way we interpret this trait in column 2.

Selfishness	"I can't be wrong—I'm too important."
Pride	"I've been hurt." (Self is important.)
Unbiblical, unrealistic view of self	"I enjoy getting attention from others by playing up the wrong."
Self-pity	"Wrongs make me feel worse. I can't handle being a nobody."

There is no bargain price for forgiveness. Forgiveness cost God His Son. Forgiveness will cost us too. Forgiveness takes a personal Calvary in our daily lives. We have to die to our selfish desires. Galatians 2:20 calls this being "crucified with Christ." This is particularly true when we forgive others.

12. According to Galatians 2:20, what attitude should we have, which also applies when we forgive?

A good thing to remember when dying to self is that a dead person can't be insulted!

Key Actions

If you are a Christian with an unforgiving spirit, your unforgiveness will ruin your fellowship with God and your prayer life.

13. (a) Do you believe that God desires to forgive you of past wrongs?

    (b) Have you received God's forgiveness for sin by experiencing the new birth?

14. What does Ephesians 4:26 say about forgiveness (last phrase of the verse only)?

Don't wait to forgive—do not delay! Some people are unwilling to forgive offenders until they have roasted the offenders for a while. The offended people want some satisfaction from the wrong committed against them. This reaction is not good. Retribution only deepens the wound.

15. Read Luke 17:3 and 4.
    (a) Summarize what Jesus was teaching about forgiveness in these verses.

    (b) How are we to deal with someone who offends us seven times (or more) in one day and each time asks for forgiveness?

God forgives us each time we ask Him. He also forgives us freely and completely. We are to treat others the same way.

16. Read Hebrews 8:12.

    (a) What does God do when He forgives us?

    (b) How should we forgive others?

Don't keep bringing up past wrongs. One man said, "Every time my wife and I get into an argument, she gets historical." His friend corrected him by saying, "You mean hysterical." "No," said the first man, "I mean historical. Every time we get into an argument, she brings up everything I've ever done."

No one ever said that forgiveness is easy. Forgiveness is hard, but the rewards are great.

Locking God's Truths into Our Hearts

⚷ *Be sure that you have experienced God's forgiveness and have become His child (Romans 10:13).* Have you done this?

⚷ *Confess to God your unforgiving spirit—acknowledge it as sin.*

⚷ *Recognize that any problem (whether it involves a person or a situation) may be a tool of God in your life.* God may use a problem to refine you and help you become more like Him.

⚷ *Release the offender in an act of the will: choose to forgive the debt or wrong.*

O━🔑 *Refocus on God's forgiveness of your wrongs (Ephesians 4:32).*

O━🔑 *Rely on God for victory over an unforgiving spirit.* See Romans 5:5 and Philippians 4:13.

O━🔑 *If necessary, do a "forgiveness" activity.* Write a heart-to-heart letter to someone who has hurt you, and instead of mailing the letter, destroy it.

O━🔑 *Thank God for helping you forgive.* You will know that you have forgiven when past incidents no longer sting you as badly as they once did, the grudge you had been carrying has been lifted, and your spirit has been renewed.

Love, the Mark of True Christianity

Key Word: Love

"For God so loved the world, that he gave his only begotten Son, that whosoever believeth in him should not perish, but have everlasting life" (John 3:16).

THE MOST profound truth in the universe is that God loves us just as we are, yet many people miss this truth because of its simplicity. *"God commendeth his love toward us*, in that, while we were yet sinners, Christ died for us. . . . *When we were enemies,* we were reconciled to God by the death of his Son" (Romans 5:8, 10; emphasis added).

God's love is outwardly focused toward others (not inwardly focused on Himself). His love is utterly unselfish. This kind of love is found only in God. It does not come naturally to any of us. So only God can help us set aside our own desires and instincts; only He enables us to practice His kind of love—the kind that gives but expects nothing in return. This love, called agape love, is described in 1 Corinthians 13.

Unlocking the Truths about Love

1. Read John 13:34 and 35.
   (a) What new commandment did Jesus provide?

   (b) What is an identifying mark of a Christian (v. 35)?

The command was new because it refers to a special love among believers based on the love of Jesus Christ for them. True Christians show forth Christ's love by their love for one another.

Love is connected to all of our relationships. The quality of our love translates into the way we treat others. This is particularly true in our family relationships, for it is in our families that we expose our true selves. We can say we love God; but if we mistreat our family, our actions say *we do not!*

We are to demonstrate God's love beyond our family members. Romans 13:10 states that we are to love our neighbors.

2. What is the other purpose of love found in Romans 13:8?

Read Galatians 5:22 and 23. "The word 'fruit' is singular, indicating that these qualities constitute a unity, all of which should be found in a believer who lives under the control of the Spirit. In an ultimate sense this 'fruit' is simply the life of Christ lived out in a Christian" *(The Bible Knowledge Commentary: New Testament,* 608).

3. Reread Galatians 5:22 and 23.
   (a) What is the first virtue mentioned?

(b) How does this quality relate to all the others?

4. Read Ephesians 5:1 and 2.
   (a) What does verse 1 tell us to be?

   (b) What example of love did Christ set for us?

   (c) How can we follow this example? (The word "walk" has the meaning of "living"; it refers to our lifestyle.)

What Is Love?

5. What attribute of God is mentioned in 1 John 4:8?

6. In 1 John 4:7 and 8 the words "love" and "loveth" appear five times. What five things does this passage say about love?
   (a)

   (b)

(c)

(d)

(e)

We are to love because God is love and love is "of God." If we don't love, we're not of Him. But what does the Bible mean when it talks about this kind of love? As we noticed in an earlier lesson, it often helps to define what something *is not* so that we have a better idea of what it *is*. Let's look at four kinds of human love that God's love *is not*.

⇨ It is not *romantic love*.

⇨ It is not merely *emotional love* (a tingly sensation or sentimentalism).

⇨ It is not *ecumenical love* (a friendly spirit of tolerance regardless of belief).

⇨ It is not merely *charity*, or pity (such as giving to some charitable organization).

God not only tells us to love, but He also shows us how to love.

7. Read John 15:13 and 14.
   (a) How did God's Son, Jesus Christ, demonstrate His love to us?

   (b) How should we respond to His love?

8. Let's look at one of the most familiar verses in the Bible about love, John 3:16.
   (a) What action did God take toward the world?

   (b) To what degree did He take this action?

   (c) What did His action accomplish?

   (d) Have you believed in His Son? Are you telling others about His love?

Qualities of Love

In 1 Corinthians 13 the apostle Paul personified love; that is, he represented love as a person, or as having human qualities. Christ is the perfection of each of these qualities. He wants to work these qualities through our lives as we yield to the Holy Spirit's control. Let's look at them individually.

Love Is Patient. "Charity [love] suffereth long" (1 Corinthians 13:4). The Greek word used for long-suffering has the idea of patience with people. It is the word used of the person who is wronged and easily has it within her power to avenge herself but doesn't. The quality of patience (long-suffering) is not common to our fallen nature.

Love Is Kind. "Charity [love] . . . is kind" (1 Corinthians 13:4). Kindness is the other side of patience. Patience endures injuries from others, while kindness pays them back with good deeds. Christ said, "Love your enemies, . . . do good to them" (Matthew 5:44).

9. The book of Proverbs has a few things to say about kindness. Read the following verses and answer the questions.
    (a) In Proverbs 11:17 the term "merciful man" really means "kind man." According to this verse, why should we practice kindness?

    (b) According to Proverbs 12:25, what is another benefit of kindness? (The term "good word" means "kind word.")

Proverbs 25:21 and 22 say, "If thine enemy be hungry, give him bread to eat; and if he be thirsty, give him water to drink: for thou shalt heap coals of fire upon his head, and the LORD shall reward thee."

Heaping coals on someone's head wasn't an act of retribution; it was an act of kindness. If a person's fire went out, she would need to borrow some live coals to restart her fire. Giving her coals in a pan to carry home was a kindness. And in the East, the woman would carry the coals in a pan on her head. So even when our enemies treat us poorly, we need to repay them with kindness.

Love Is Not Envious. "Charity [love] envieth not" (1 Corinthians 13:4). Envy, as used in verse 4, refers to the sin of jealousy. Solomon called envy the "rottenness of the bones" (Proverbs 14:30).

Jealousy seems to be two-layered. The first layer is superficial. It says, "I want what you have." The second layer is deep-rooted jealousy that says, "I wish you didn't have it."

10. What does James 3:16 say about envy?

11. How can the teachings about love in 1 Corinthians 13 help us defeat envy or jealousy?

Love Does Not Boast. "Charity [love] vaunteth not itself" (1 Corinthians 13:4). "Vaunteth" means "to make a vain display of one's own worth or attainments"; "to brag." Bragging, or boasting, is the speech or action of pride. It is interesting that the Greek word translated "boast" comes from a root word meaning "windbag." Love is not a "windbag," shooting off its mouth about her own accomplishments. Love is not chatter designed to make one person look better than another.

Boasting is the flipside of envy. Envy wants what others have. Boasting is an attempt to make other people want what we have. Also, the desire of boastfulness is the opposite of the purpose of love. Boasting is geared to hurt others. Its purpose is to make the boaster stand out and others to feel inferior. Boasting is natural to the carnal, sinful nature. How do we defeat it? We defeat it by following the example of our Savior.

12. Read John 12:49.
    (a) What example did the Savior provide?

    (b) How can we imitate His example?

Love Is Not Proud (or, literally, "conceited," which is the attitude of pride). "Charity [love] . . . is not puffed up" (1 Corinthians 13:4).

13. Read Proverbs 8:13. When we fear the Lord (respect Him and try to please Him), how will we feel about pride and related sins?

The difference between love and conceit is that conceit is "big-headed," while love is "big-hearted." Conceit says, "I want everyone to focus on me"; love says, "I want to encourage you and focus more on you."

Love Is Not Rude. "[Love] doth not behave itself unseemly" (1 Corinthians 13:5). The Greek word translated "unseemly" in English means "rudely." It is the opposite of behaving with courtesy. Rudeness is an action that says to a person, "I don't love you, and I could care less what affects you. I will do what I want." Rudeness is doing the wrong thing at the right time. Courtesy, on the other hand, is love's system for conduct.

First Corinthians 14:40 commands believers to do things in a fitting, orderly manner, which means showing *courtesy* instead of *rudeness.* Courtesy is simple; we express it in little, often overlooked ways. A woman does not need a great education or skill to be courteous. Courtesy goes out of its way to do little things for others.

Love Is Not Self-seeking. "[Love] seeketh not her own" (1 Corinthians 13:5). Love does not pursue selfish advantage. Love does not desire or seek its own praise, honor, profit, or pleasure. Selfishness comes from an inflated view of our own importance. Instead of being *self-centered,* God wants us to show His love by being *God-centered.*

14. Read Romans 15:1 and 2. When we live a God-centered life, how can we show God's love to others?

Love Is Not Easily Angered. "[Love] is not easily provoked" (1 Corinthians 13:5). In other words, love does not lose its cool. The word "anger" comes from a word that means "a sudden outburst." Anger is connected to self-centeredness. People easily become angry when someone, especially someone close to them, blocks their goals. Anger results in harmful words and actions that may never be forgotten.

15. What do the following verses say about controlling anger?
    (a) Proverbs 15:18

    (b) Proverbs 19:11

Love Keeps No Record of Wrongs. "[Love] thinketh no evil" (1 Corinthians 13:5). This description has the idea of keeping track of wrongs, like a bookkeeper's recording numbers in a ledger so she won't forget them. Love never keeps books on someone else's evil and never runs a record of another's offenses. Love just forgives and seeks to forget. Love controls its thoughts.

16. Read Proverbs 23:7 and 25:28. Why is it important to "[think] no evil"?

Love Does Not Delight in Evil. "[Love] rejoiceth not in iniquity" (1 Corinthians 13:6). Bad news travels fast because people naturally love to rejoice in the bad. God's love is saddened when it hears of defeats and tragedies in other people's lives. It is easy to be glad at other people's problems, especially if they make us look better. Christians ought not allow themselves to rejoice in the pitfalls of others.

17. Read 3 John 4, 1 Peter 4:8, and Ephesians 4:29.
    (a) What should cause us to rejoice (3 John 4)?

    (b) What does 1 Peter 4:8 command us to do? Why?

    (c) What warning did Paul give in Ephesians 4:29?

It is a joy to see both our physical and spiritual children walking with God. But when they sin, we're to "cover" the sin in love. To cover someone's sin means not to broadcast it to others. How much of our conversation would be silenced if we never talked about others' failures, faults, or sins? Christian parents ought to be careful about making critical comments in the presence of their children.

Key Actions

Love Protects. "[Love] beareth all things" (1 Corinthians 13:7). "Beareth," or "bears," means "covers with silence," implying protection; it also means "suffers." In Romans 15:1 the word "bear" has the idea of sufferings "borne" on behalf of others. So love protects those she loves and even suffers on their behalf.

In practical terms, bearing with a weaker or newer Christian means helping her learn how to study the Bible and pray, helping her get to know other Christians who could help her, and helping her get acquainted with the church and pastor.

Love Trusts. "Believeth all things" (1 Corinthians 13:7). We must put our trust in the right place. People fail and disappoint us from time to time.

18. Romans 4:1–21 gives the wonderful account of Abraham's relationship with God.
    (a) Why did Abraham trust God (v. 21)?

    (b) What happens in our lives when we trust God to do what He has promised?

Love Hopes. "[Love] hopeth all things" (1 Corinthians 13:7). Romans 8:24 and Hebrew 11:1 speak of having hope and faith.

19. Share a time when you had great faith and hope and how God rewarded your faith and hope in Him.

Love Perseveres. "[Love] endureth all things" (1 Corinthians 13:7). In other words, love remains steadfast even in unpleasant situations, even when people are unpleasant.

Locking God's Truths into Our Hearts

Think of ways you possess and practice love. Read Romans 5:5. The distinctive mark of a dedicated Christian is love, as expressed in self-sacrificial action. Are you practicing it?

The Holy Spirit comes to live within us the moment we receive Christ as Savior. Are you allowing God's forgiving love (the kind referred to in Ephesians 4:32) to help you love others?

Everyone needs love. Do you express your love for others (including family) by acts of kindness? Do you offer help before you are asked? Are you interested in doing "little things" for people? Are you quick to give an approving smile or an encouraging word to others?

Remember God's goodness to you and learn to be content with God's blessing in your life. First Corinthians 3:3 lists the characteristics of a carnal Christian and mentions envy (jealousy) first. How do you deal with envy or jealousy? This sin must be renounced. Pray every day for whoever stirs up envy in your heart. Rekindle God's love in your heart and decide to love others.

God's love leaves no room for pride in our hearts. Most people have a great need to deal with the sin of self-boasting. Willingly humble yourself to God in attitude and action. Give God the glory due Him, and be thankful. Humility is the key to a close walk with God. It is the key to usefulness for Him. Can you say at the end of the day, "God, I have not boasted about myself today, but I've tried to bring glory to Your name"?

🔑 *Getting rid of selfishness will transform your life.* Love "doth not behave itself unseemly, seeketh not her own." Literally, love does not insist upon its own way. Love is not selfish. (Motherhood is a great example of selflessness.) Do you always have to have your own way, or are you practicing unselfishness?

🔑 *Loving means not losing your temper; it means exercising self-control.* When we let our tempers fly, we are not acting in love. Don't say, "I'm a Christian; I couldn't get angry." Don't repress or express anger; confess it—confess it as sin, a costly sin. Unconfessed unrighteous anger can cost you your mate, your children, your job, your health, and, worst of all, your fellowship with God.

🔑 *Love does not think evil.* Love involves right thinking. Rightful thinking will govern our speech, guard our sight (sight affects our thoughts), and guide our steps. Examine your thoughts, and exchange wrong thoughts for right ones. Dedicate your mind to love God with all of your heart and soul and strength. Decide to exercise proper thinking. Expect God to bless!

LEADER'S GUIDE

Suggestions for Leaders

The effectiveness of a group Bible study usually depends on two things: (1) the leader herself and (2) the ladies' commitment to prepare beforehand and interact during the study. You cannot totally control the second factor, but you have total control over the first one. These brief suggestions will help you be an effective Bible study leader.

You will want to prepare each lesson a week in advance. During the week, read supplemental material and look for illustrations in the everyday events of your life as well as in the lives of others.

Encourage the ladies in the Bible study to complete each lesson before the meeting itself. This preparation will make the discussion more interesting. You can suggest that ladies answer two or three questions a day as part of their daily Bible reading time rather than trying to do the entire lesson at one sitting.

The physical setting in which you meet will have some bearing on the study itself. An informal circle of chairs, chairs around a table, someone's living room or family room—these types of settings encourage people to relax and participate. In addition to an informal setting, create an atmosphere in which ladies feel free to participate and be themselves.

During the discussion time, here are a few things to observe:

• Don't do all the talking. This is not designed to be a lecture.

• Encourage discussion on each question by adding ideas and questions.

• Don't discuss controversial issues that will divide the group. (Differences of opinion are healthy; divisions are not.)

• Don't allow one lady to dominate the discussion. Use statements such as these to draw others into the study: "Let's hear from someone on this side of the room" (the side opposite the dominant talker); "Let's hear from someone who has not shared yet today."

• Stay on the subject. The tendency toward tangents is always possible in a discussion. One of your responsibilities as the leader is to keep the group on track.

• Don't get bogged down on a question that interests only one person.

You may want to use the last fifteen minutes of the scheduled time for prayer. If you have a large group of ladies, divide into smaller groups for prayer. You could call this the "Share and Care Time."

If you have a morning Bible study, encourage the ladies to go out for lunch with someone else from time to time. This is a good way to get acquainted with new ladies. Occasionally you could plan a time when ladies bring their own lunches or salads to share and eat together. These things help promote fellowship and friendship in the group.

The formats that follow are suggestions only. You can plan your own format, use one of these, or adapt one of these to your needs.

2-hour Bible Study

10:00—10:15   Coffee and fellowship time
10:15—10:30   Get-acquainted time
              Have two ladies take five minutes each to tell something about themselves and their families.
              Also use this time to make announcements and, if appropriate, take an offering for the babysitters.
10:30—11:45   Bible study
              Leader guides discussion of the questions in the day's lesson.
11:45—12:00   Prayer time

2-hour Bible Study

10:00—10:45   Bible lesson
              Leader teaches a lesson on the content of the material. No discussion during this time.
10:45—11:00   Coffee and fellowship
11:00—11:45   Discussion time
              Divide into small groups with an appointed leader for each group. Discuss the questions in the day's lesson.
11:45—12:00   Prayer time

1½-hour Bible Study

10:00—10:30   Bible study
              Leader guides discussion of half the questions in the day's lesson.
10:30—10:45   Coffee and fellowship
10:45—11:15   Bible study
              Leader continues discussion of the questions in the day's lesson.
11:15—11:30   Prayer time

Answers for Leader's Use

Lesson 1

1. We're not to go to bed without first resolving the issues that caused anger.
2. We give the Devil a foothold, an opportunity to control our lives.
3. (a) Unwholesome words. (b) Build up and benefit them.
4. On being kind, compassionate, and forgiving toward others, just like God forgave us.
5. We should avoid letting ourselves become angry ("cease from anger"). We are to use self-control to turn away from anger. We should not fret, because fretting ends only in evil.
6. (a) She is wise and is careful about what she says, using knowledge to

respond rightly to people. (b) A person who is quickly angry reacts foolishly. She uses harsh words, making people angrier, and she responds
without thought of the results.

7. Stir up anger: wrong words destroy and crush our spirits and alienate
   those around us. Downplay anger: right words ease anger. They are
   emotionally healing. They add quality to our lives.

8. (a) To overlook it. We should disregard transgressions that could oth-
   erwise make us angry. (b) Personal answers.

9. If the cause of anger is not quickly mended, the problem will grow larger
   and larger until it breaks open and the anger pours out. Contention
   needs to be ended immediately because great feuds can develop from
   insignificant causes. It is best to drop contentious matters immediately
   before they become uncontrollable.

10. (a) God's punishment. (b) Angry people just keep repeating their angry
    actions because they never learn to control their temper. If you help an
    angry person one time, you'll probably have to help many times.

11. There is more hope for a fool than for a person who speaks without
    giving thought to her words.

12. (a) A wrathful (hot-tempered) person and a patient person. (b) The first
    responds to life by stirring up trouble; the second responds to life by
    calming bad situations.

13. Angry people. We should not choose friends who are hot-tempered
    and easily angered because they will influence us to become just like
    them.

14. Peacemakers.

15. (a) A fool and a prudent man. (b) The fool loses his temper quickly, and
    everyone knows it. The prudent man controls his response to an insult,
    including forgiving it.

16. (a) Quick to listen, slow to reply, and slow to become angry. (b) Because
    these things will help us live righteously as God wants us to live.

17. He recommended not becoming angry quickly, because hasty anger
    characterizes fools.

18. She would not repay evil for evil. She would try to do what is right and
    live at peace with others. She would not give others "a taste of their
    own medicine." She would look to God to deal with others and not try
    to get revenge for herself. She would seek to overcome evil by doing
    good to others.

19. Don't let evil overtake you, but become victorious over evil by doing
    good to others.

20. Personal answers.

Lesson 2

1. (a) He hated life. He found his work burdensome. (b) Because everything
   was meaningless to him.

2. (a) Merriment and pleasure. (b) He found it meaningless.

3. (a) Achievement in building and in acquiring servants and possessions.

(b) Solomon became great and wealthy.
4. He acquired anything he wanted.
5. As meaningless and unprofitable.
6. It asks what good is it to gain everything on earth but to lose the only thing that will go into eternity—the soul.
7. Guidance, joy, God's presence.
8. That there is a proper time and season for every legitimate responsibility (time with God, time with family and friends, time for work responsibilities). We need to find the right time to do it. We get into trouble when we overload our lives with nonessentials.
9. (a, b) Personal answers.
10. It warns us not to say things that displease God and things that we will regret later. Be careful not to speak before you think. Don't whine and complain about things. Don't talk too much.
11. Don't foolishly make promises to God that you can't keep or have no intention of keeping. Promises to God are a serious matter, and we should fulfill them without delay.
12. Joy. Don't become so burdened down with life that you don't enjoy it with your mate. Love your mate. Enjoy the time God gives you together.
13. They teach us to keep focused on the work that God has given us. We're to do it the best that we can (wholeheartedly) and do it for God's glory. We're to remember to honor God in all we say and do.
14. The gift of God. It is important to be thankful for the blessings God has given us to enjoy. (Don't feel that you always need to apologize for nice things God has given you or explain the good deal you got so your fellow Christians won't be jealous.)
15. (a) To remember God (live for Him) when we are young. (b) We'll be unfulfilled and will have wasted our years and have many regrets.

Lesson 3
1. (a) She has a new life (spiritual life). She changes from an old life to a new life. (b) Yes. God says that we can *know* we have eternal life.
2. We become a new spiritual creation. We change by receiving a new set of values because the old is gone and the new has come.
3. (a) Darkness and light. (b) We should respond by having goodness, righteousness, and truth as part of our lifestyle.
4. Negative: get rid of such things as malice, guile (deceit), hypocrisies, evil speaking (slander). Positive: desire reading and studying the Bible the way a baby desires milk.
5. (a) God doesn't lie or change His mind. If He says He'll do something, He does it. (b) Jesus stays the same in the past, present, and future.
6. Because Jacob had tricked him into giving up his birthright and had tricked Isaac into giving Jacob the greater blessing.
7. (a, b) Personal answers.
8. A Man appeared to Jacob and attacked him. Jacob struggled with the Man until daybreak and would not let go until He blessed Jacob.

9. God.
10. (a) His name from Jacob to Israel (meaning God fights). (b) From that day on, Jacob walked with a limp.
11. (a) Obedience. (b) Samuel viewed disobedience as rebellion against God and rejection of God's word.
12. We give God control of our lives when we allow Him to guide us. This means we do not try to figure out things ourselves; instead we follow God's leading. It means changing because we have God's power helping us and we are not relying on our own determination and willpower.
13. God will direct the paths of their lives.
14. The Man's blessing.
15. (a) Yes, of course. (b) He wanted to teach Jacob a lesson. (It's a lesson for us too.) (c) Some of the lessons God wants to teach us are of His greatness and power, to submit to His will for peace and blessing, and that His will is best for our lives.
16. Personal answers.
17. (a) Stand firm for God, not letting anything move you. Give yourself wholeheartedly to the work of God. (b) Our labor for God is not meaningless; it counts!
18. Personal answers.
19. (a) Acknowledge your sins. (b) Forgive.
20. God's Word.

Lesson 4
1. (a) A command is an order to do something without questioning. A suggestion is more of an option that you can do or you may choose not to do. (b) Have faith in God.
2. To believe without doubting.
3. We are to pray believing as if we have already received the answer to our prayers.
4. (a) Assurance of what you hoped for; (b) being certain of things you cannot see.
5. We must believe that nothing is impossible with God.
6. (a) Like a tree planted by water whose roots spread into the river for moisture. This person will not fear when adversity comes but will keep trusting the Lord and yielding spiritual fruit. (b) Choosing to worry instead of trusting God.
7. God forgives us when we acknowledge, uncover, and confess our sins to Him (cf. 1 John 1:9).
8. (a) He rebuked them for claiming Him as their Lord but not doing what He said. (b) We should do what He says; that is, obey.
9. We are saved by grace through faith—not by our own works but as a gift from God. If we could do anything (works) to save ourselves, then we could boast about it.
10. They were healed and their lives were changed because of their faith in Jesus.

11. (a) She had no money, and her creditors were going to take her sons as slaves. (b) To Elisha, God's prophet. (c) He told her to borrow empty pots (containers) from her neighbors, pour the oil into them, and sell the oil. (d) Her faith caused her to do as Elisha said. She borrowed every pot she could, and the oil didn't run out until she had used the last pot (v. 6). She sold the oil and made enough to pay off her creditors.
12. No one else, even in Israel, had that man's "so great faith."
13. Martha: because she was worried about the cares of life. Mary: because she listened to Him.
14. Fear.
15. Doubt.
16. Human reasoning. They reasoned among themselves, trying to figure out a spiritual lesson (v. 6) from a human viewpoint (v. 7).
17. The example of their suffering and perseverance should motivate us to get rid of sin and anything that hinders us spiritually so that we can run the race for Christ with excellence.
18. We get spiritual exercise by running the prescribed "race" God has for us and by running with patience and perseverance.
19. On Jesus.

Lesson 5
1. (a) Being tempted of the serpent, they sinned to satisfy their own self-will. (b) Guilty and ashamed, but they blamed others for their sin. They felt separated from God. (c) They were made to leave the Garden. The woman was to experience pain and suffering in childbirth, and she had to submit to her husband. The man was to experience hardship in growing food to eat. They both were to experience hardships and death.
2. Because everyone has sinned. God is holy; our sin is against Him. We need His forgiveness.
3. (a) No one is righteous. We all commit wrongs (sin), so we need to be forgiven. (b) Some possible answers are feelings of hurt, anger, disappointment, distrust, or guilt. (c) Forgiveness and cancellation of the trespass will restore the previous relationship.
4. Christ forgave those who nailed Him to the cross even though they didn't ask for forgiveness. He set the example for forgiveness. We should forgive others as He forgives us.
5. Iniquity (sin).
6. Personal answers. We should forgive because we *know* it is the right thing to do, not because we feel like it (our feelings change).
7. (a) Reminding offenders of their offenses can open old wounds and stir up more trouble, especially if they did not realize they had offended us. (b) Not talking about the offense to others keeps us from thinking too much about it; it minimizes the offense instead of maximizing it. (c) It keeps us from dwelling on the offense and living it over and over. The more we think about it, the worse it seems.
8. Personal answers, but here are some suggestions: Rule 1—People with

rigid rules are offended when their rules are not followed. We cannot control (nor should we try to control) others' behavior. When we follow this rule, we are hurt and offended less. Rule 2—Trying to understand why another person did something helps ease the pain of the hurt. Rule 3—Don't blame someone else for all of your troubles. Accept the person, forgive him/her, and move on.

9. When: when we have a quarrel with another. Why: Christ forgave us.
10. $1,000.
11. Selfishness: "I've been hurt." (Self is important.) Pride: "I can't be wrong— I'm too important." Unbiblical, unrealistic view of self: "Wrongs make me feel worse. I can't handle being a nobody." Self-pity: "I enjoy getting attention from others by playing up the wrong."
12. We should have an attitude of being dead to our sinful selves, including unforgiveness. And we should let Christ live through us.
13. (a, b) Personal answers.
14. Forgive right away; don't put it off until the next day.
15. (a) Christ forgives us when we ask Him. He doesn't make us do penance or wait until later; He forgives us quickly, freely, and fully. (b) We are to forgive those who ask to be forgiven.
16. (a) He forgives our sins and remembers them no more. (b) We should do the same for others.

Lesson 6
1. (a) To love other Christians. (b) Love for other Christians.
2. Love helps us fulfill God's law.
3. (a) Love. It is the foundation of the other virtues. (b) When God's love permeates our lives, we will naturally overflow with the other qualities of the fruit of the Spirit. Joy, peace, longsuffering, gentleness, goodness, faith, meekness, and temperance express love.
4. (a) Followers of Jesus Christ. (b) He gave Himself as a sacrifice for our sins by dying on the cross for us. (c) We follow Christ's example when our lifestyle (walk) is saturated with the love of Christ. (He is our example of love.) How we treat others mirrors our relationship with Christ.
5. Love.
6. (a) We are to love one another. (b) Love comes from God. (c) Loving shows that a person has been born of God. (d) Loving shows that a person knows God; lack of love shows that a person does not know God. (e) God is love.
7. (a) He gave His life for us on the cross when He died for our sins. (b) By accepting Christ as our Savior and by telling others of His great love.
8. (a) He loved the world. (b) To the degree that He gave His only Son to die for us. (c) It provides everlasting life with Him in Heaven. (d) Personal answers.
9. (a) Showing kindness is good for us. (b) Kind words cheer the heart— ours and the hearts of others.
10. It is accompanied by evil work, or practice, and confusion.

11. We should love one another according to 1 Corinthians 13. If we truly love someone, we are not jealous of him/her.
12. (a) He did not speak of Himself but of God the Father. (b) By trying to bring glory to God, not to ourselves.
13. We will hate pride and the sins that accompany it.
14. We can show God's love by not looking down on or judging others who are weak. We should not try to please them by participating in their weaknesses, but we should show love to them and help them grow in the faith. We are not to please just ourselves but to please those who need help by our building them up.
15. (a) People who are quick to become angry stir up conflict, but people who are slow to become angry have a calming effect. (b) We should patiently put off becoming angry and realize that it is honorable to overlook an offense.
16. The way we think determines the way we act. When we do not use discipline to control our evil or angry thoughts, we will become vulnerable and have no self-control over our relationships with others. This results in wrong thoughts rushing into our minds without restraint. And then we are like a city with broken-down walls.
17. (a) Seeing God's children living rightly. (b) Have love among us. We are to do this because love covers a multitude of sins and helps us overlook the faults of others. It helps us love the unlovely. (c) We should speak only the things that will help others to hear God's love in us. We are to forgive others rather than to harbor ill feelings. We should not talk unrighteously about others. Instead we should say things that help build up and encourage others.
18. (a) He believed God was able to do what He had promised. (b) We have peace in storms, calmness in calamity, and hope when all seems to be lost.
19. Personal answers.